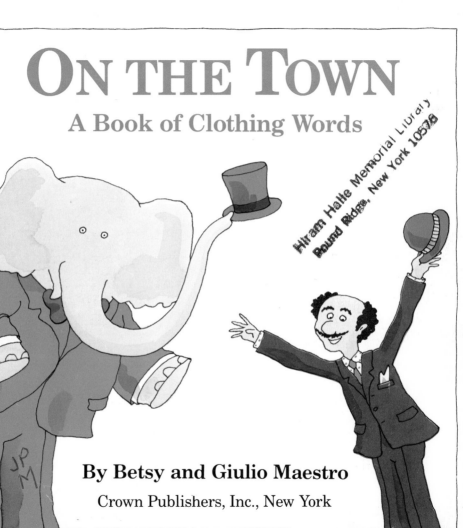

ON THE TOWN
A Book of Clothing Words

By Betsy and Giulio Maestro

Crown Publishers, Inc., New York

10 9 8 7 6 5 4 3 2 1

The text of this book was set in 24 pt. Century Expanded.
The four-color illustrations were prepared as black line and wash drawings
with line overlays prepared by the artist for pink, blue and yellow.

Library of Congress Cataloging in Publication Data
Maestro, Betsy. On the Town. Summary: Words for and pictures of the
clothing worn by a well-dressed man, woman, and elephant for
daytime and nighttime activities. 1. Clothing and dress—Juvenile
literature. [1. Clothing and dress—Pictorial works. 2. Vocabulary]
I. Maestro, Giulio. II. Title. TX340.M27 1983 646.3 83-1810
ISBN 0-517-54749-X

bathing suits

sandals

robes

underpants

undershirts

shorts

T-shirts

socks

sneakers

sweaters

pants

jackets

caps

blouses

skirts

raincoats

boots

shirts

ties

belts

suits

shoes

coats

hats

gloves

dresses

pajamas

nightshirt

slippers